POP BALLADS

16 BELOVED SONGS

ARRANGED BY PHILLIP KEVEREN

T0086845

— PIANO LEVEL —
EARLY INTERMEDIATE

ISBN 978-1-70513-709-3

HAL•LEONARD®

Visit Hal Leonard Online at
www.halleonard.com

Visit Phillip at
www.phillipkeveren.com

World headquarters, contact:
Hal Leonard
7777 West Bluemound Road
Milwaukee, WI 53213
Email: info@halleonard.com

In Europe, contact:
Hal Leonard Europe Limited
1 Red Place
London, W1K 6PL
Email: info@halleonardeurope.com

In Australia, contact:
Hal Leonard Australia Pty. Ltd.
4 Lentara Court
Cheltenham, Victoria, 3192 Australia
Email: info@halleonard.com.au

PREFACE

Popular songs are everywhere. We hear them on the radio and television and in the movies. They leak from passing cars and neighbor's parties. A reflection of the times in which they were written, they become sonic time capsules that remind us of fleeting moments in our lives. This second edition holds newer and older songs alike, all of them immensely popular in their time.

Playing popular songs at the piano can be a very satisfying experience. "I Write the Songs" was an important piece for me when I was a young piano student. I was really excited when I could play a song on my own piano that I heard on the radio every day. My now-grown children had that same sense of wonder about "My Heart Will Go On."

So have some fun and treat yourself to some great pop ballads at the piano!

Phillip Keveren

BIOGRAPHY

Phillip Keveren, a multi-talented keyboard artist and composer, writes original works in a variety of genres from piano solo to symphonic orchestra. He gives frequent concerts and workshops for teachers and their students in the United States, Canada, Europe, and Asia. Mr. Keveren holds a B.M. in composition from California State University Northridge and a M.M. in composition from the University of Southern California.

CONTENTS

ALL OF ME

Words and Music by JOHN STEPHENS
and TOBY GAD
Arranged by Phillip Keveren

What would I do with-out your smart mouth, draw-in' me
How man-y times do I have tell you, e - ven when

in and you kick-ing me out? You've got my head spin-nin',
cry-ing, you're beau-ti-ful, too? The world is beat - ing you

no kid-din'. I can't pin you down. What's go-in'
down. I'm a - round ev-'ry mood. You're my

on in that beau-ti-ful | mind? I'm on your | mag-i-cal mys-ter-y
down - fall, you're my | muse, my worst dis - | trac-tion, my rhy-thm and

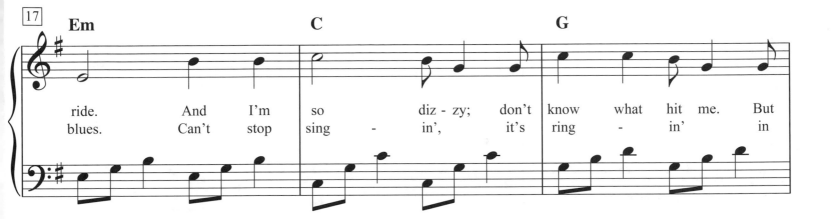

ride. And I'm | so diz - zy; don't | know what hit me. But
blues. Can't I'm stop | sing - in', it's | ring - in' in

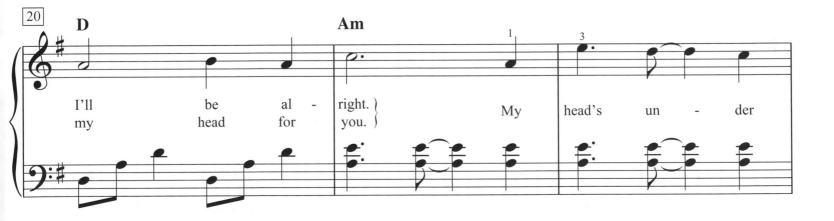

I'll be al - | right. My | head's un - der
my head for | you. |

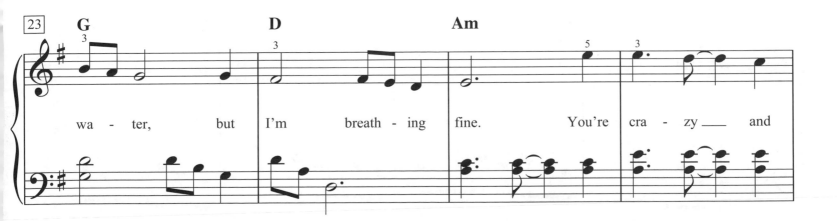

wa - ter, but I'm | breath-ing fine. | You're cra - zy and

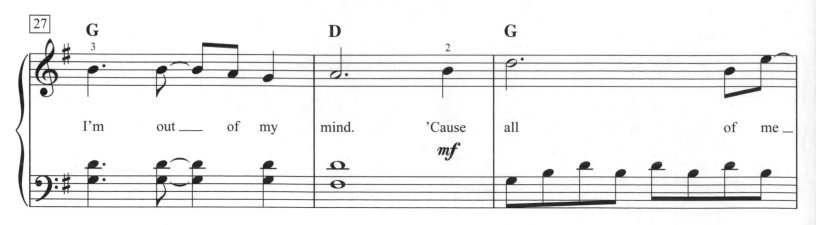

I'm out ___ of my mind. 'Cause all of me ___

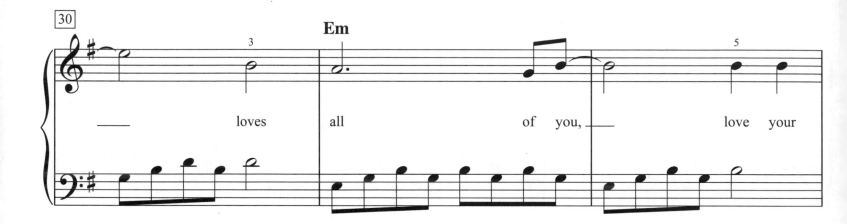

___ loves all of you, ___ love your

curves and all your edg - es, all your per - fect im - per - fec -

- tions. Give your all to me, ___ I'll give my all to you. ___

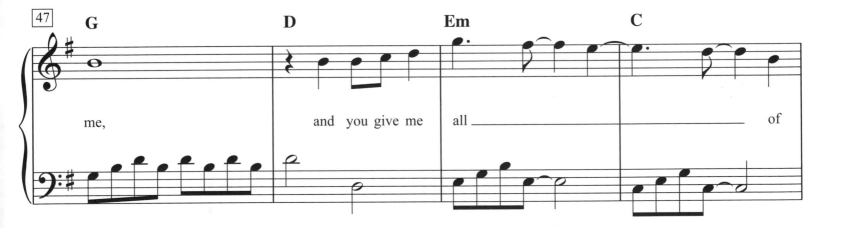

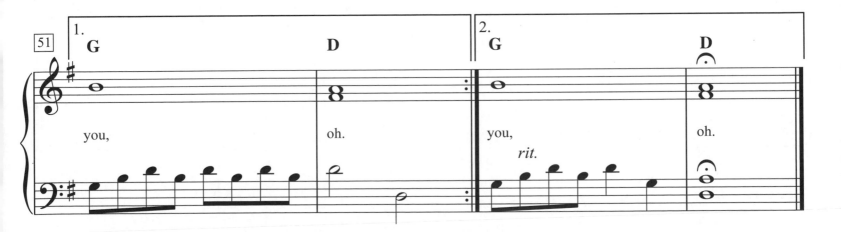

AND SO IT GOES

Words and Music by
BILLY JOEL
Arranged by Phillip Keveren

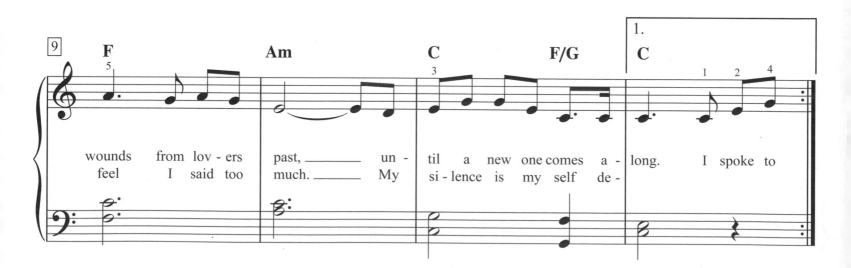

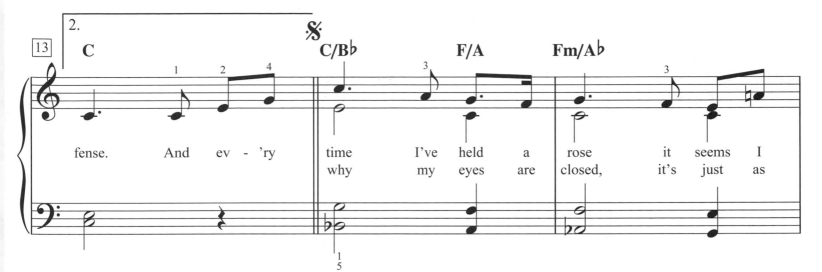

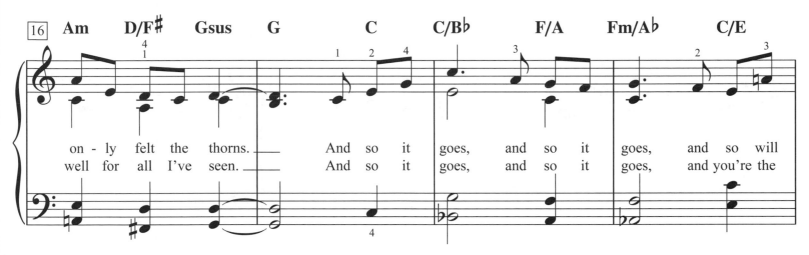

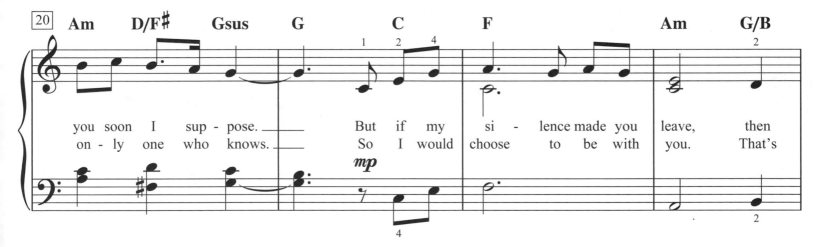

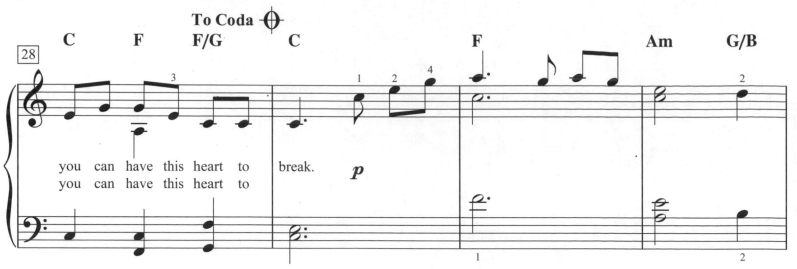

you can have this heart to break.
you can have this heart to

And this is

break.

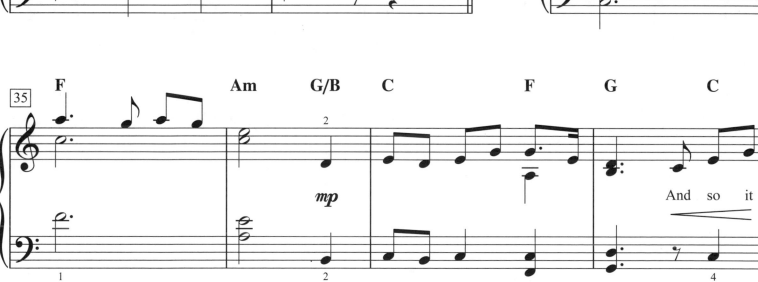

And so it

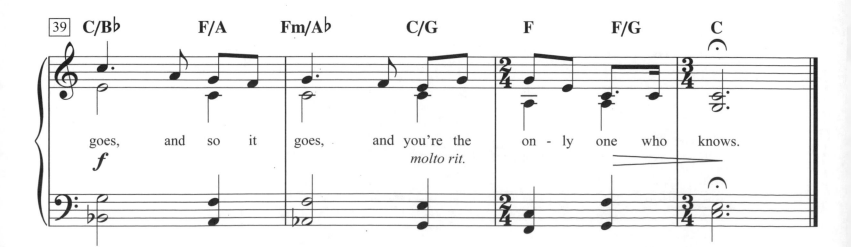

goes, and so it goes, and you're the on - ly one who knows.

ANGEL

Words and Music by
SARAH McLACHLAN
Arranged by Phillip Keveren

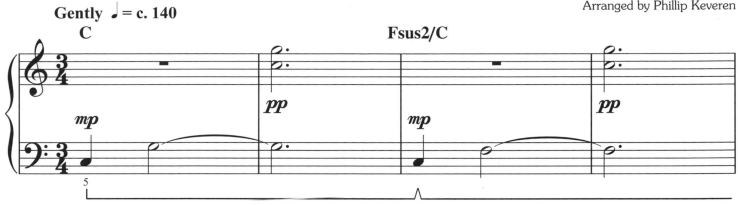

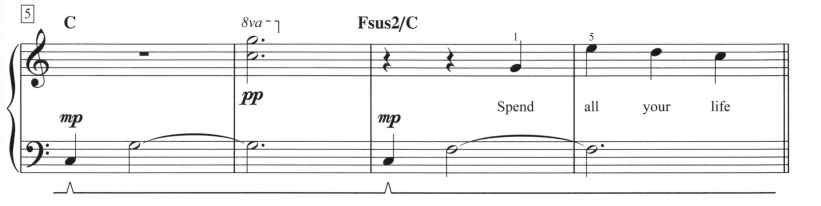

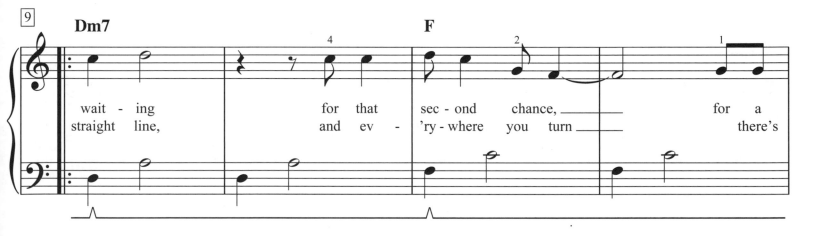

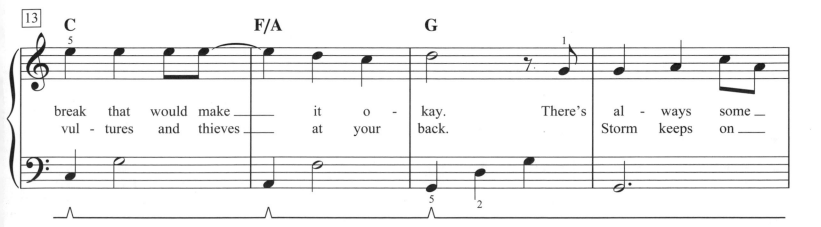

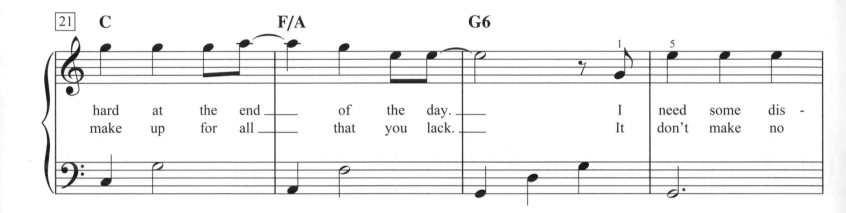

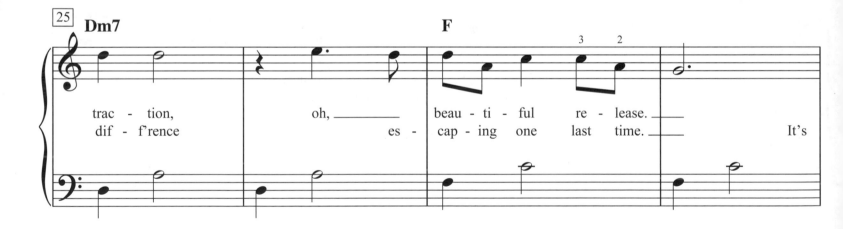

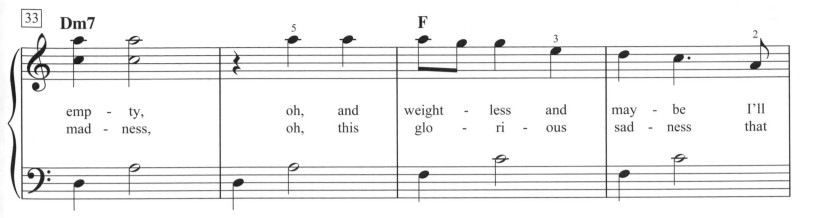

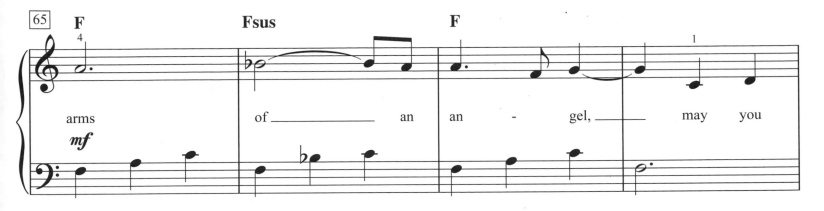

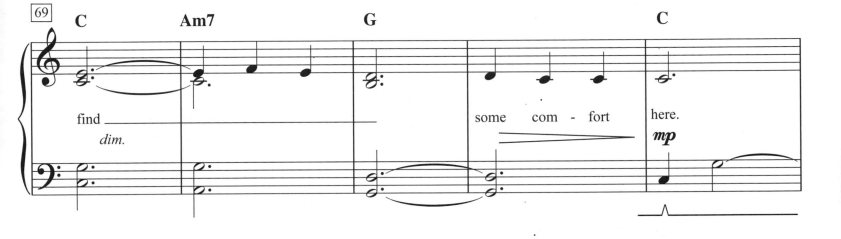

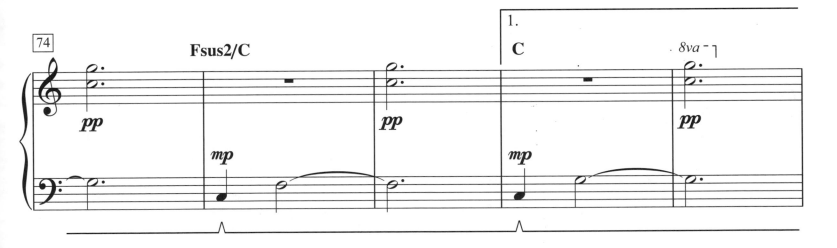

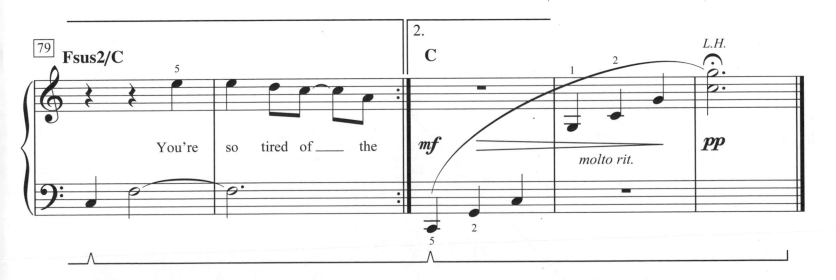

CITY OF STARS
from LA LA LAND

Music by JUSTIN HURWITZ
Lyrics by BENJ PASEK & JUSTIN PAUL
Arranged by Phillip Keveren

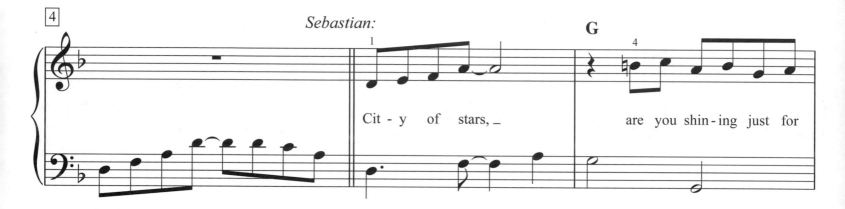

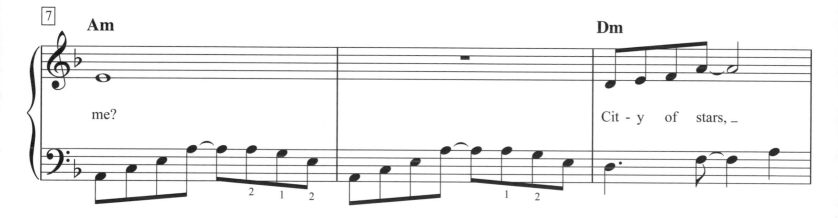

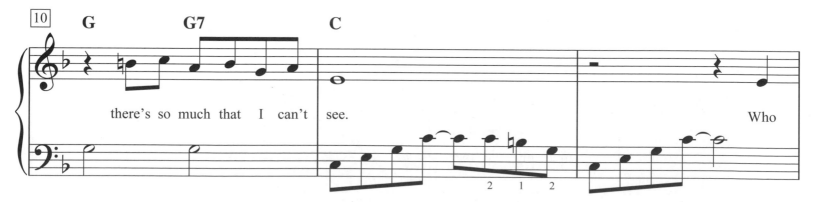

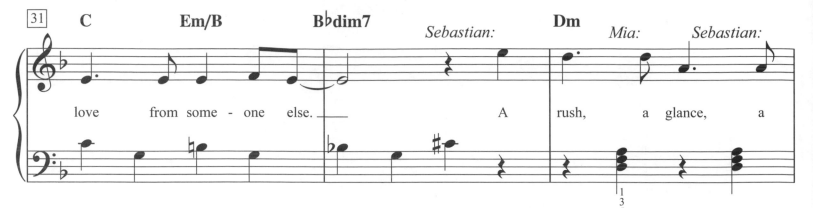

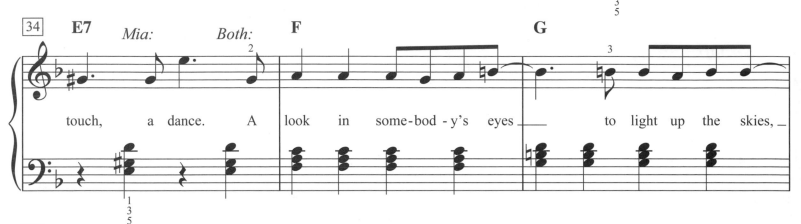

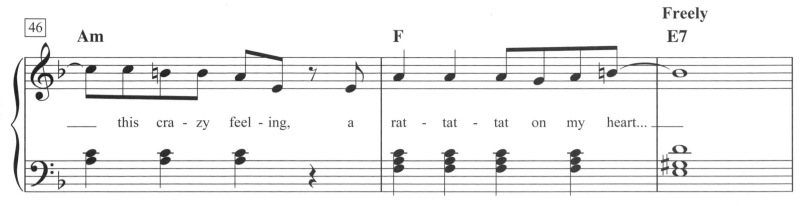

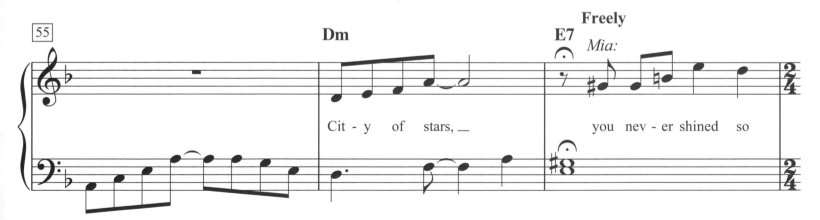

CLOCKS

Words and Music by GUY BERRYMAN,
JON BUCKLAND, WILL CHAMPION
and CHRIS MARTIN
Arranged by Phillip Keveren

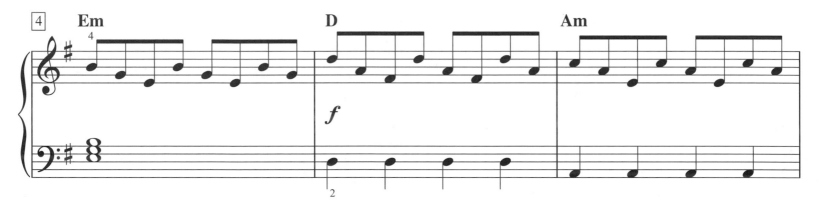

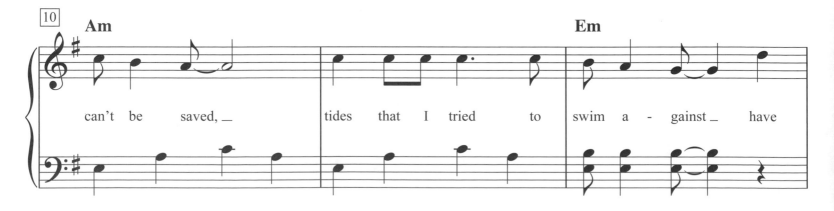

brought me down up - on my knees, __ oh, I beg, I

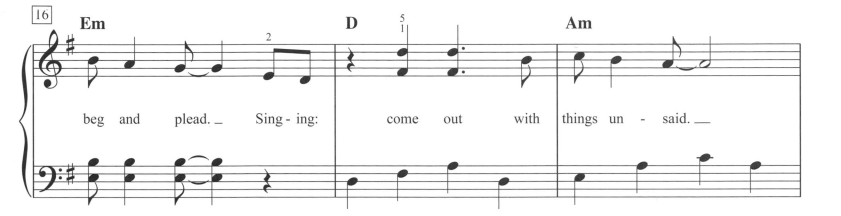

beg and plead. __ Sing - ing: come out with things un - said. __

Shoot an ap - ple off my head. __ And a trou - ble that

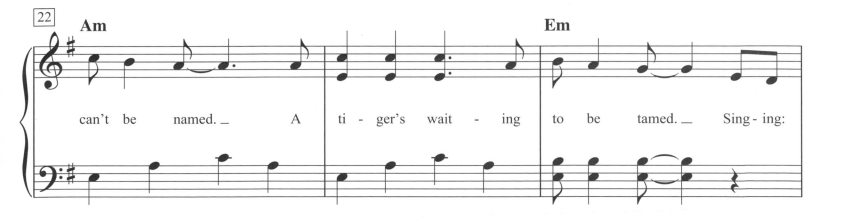

can't be named. __ A ti - ger's wait - ing to be tamed. __ Sing - ing:

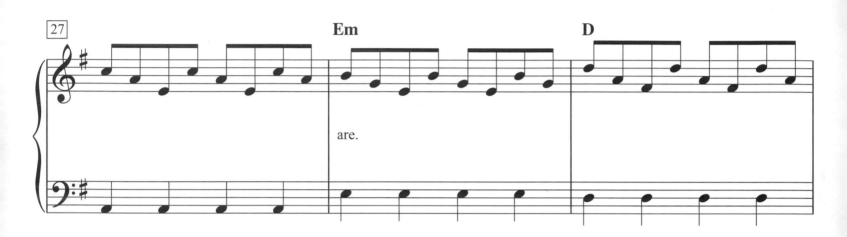

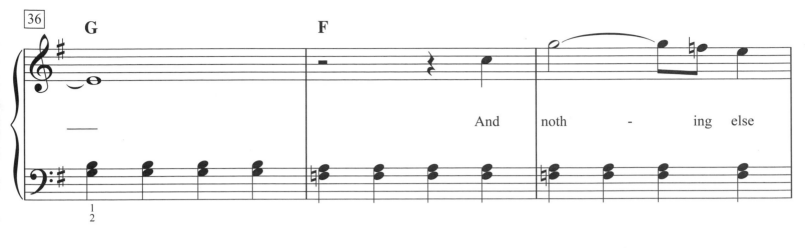

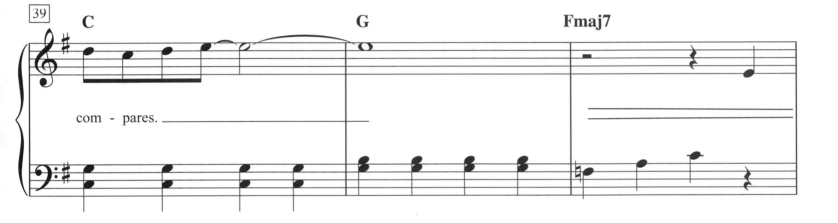

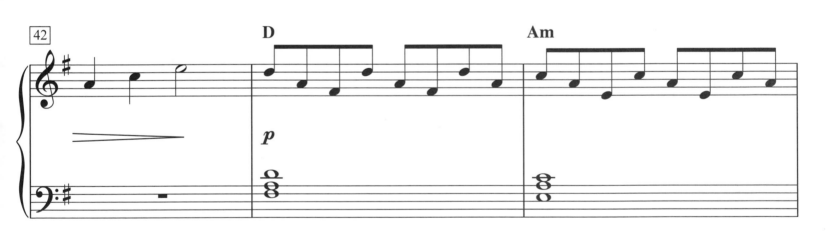

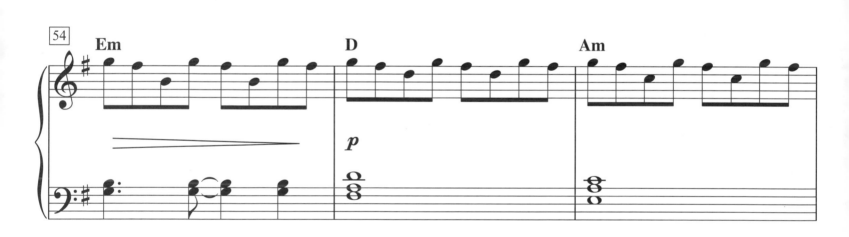

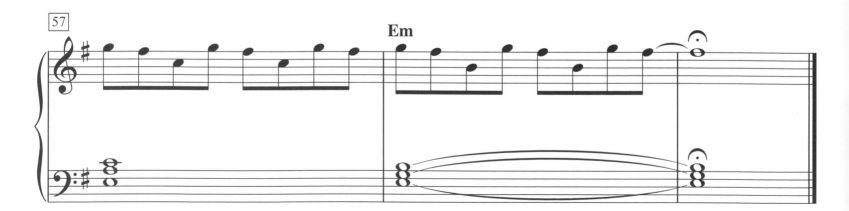

THE FIRST TIME EVER I SAW YOUR FACE

Words and Music by
EWAN MacCOLL
Arranged by Phillip Keveren

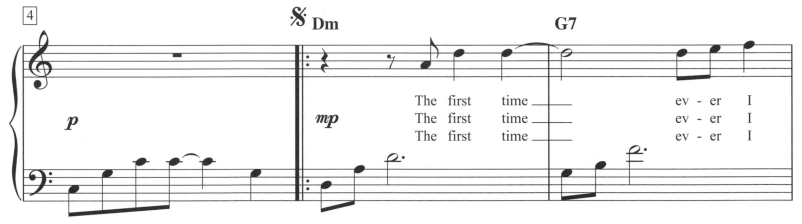

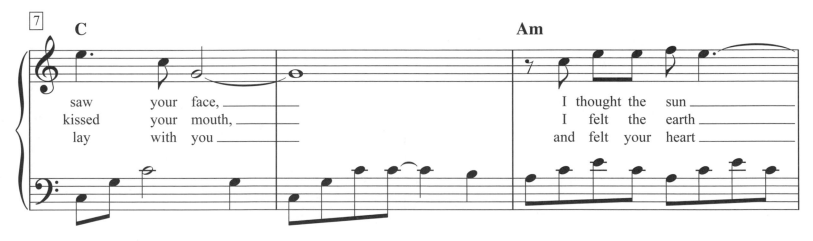

And the moon and the stars _____ were the
Like the trem - bling heart _____ of a
And I knew our joy _____ would

gifts you gave _____ to the dark _____
cap - tive bird _____ that was there _____
fill the earth _____

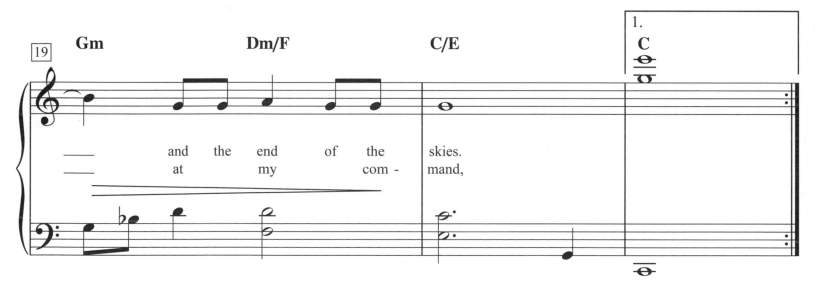

_____ and the end of the skies.
_____ at my com - mand,

my love.

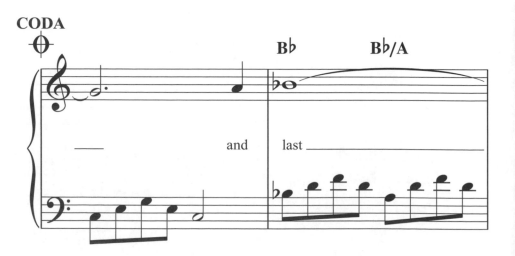

_____ and last _____

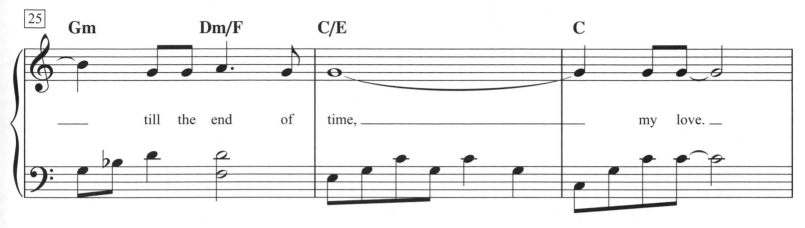

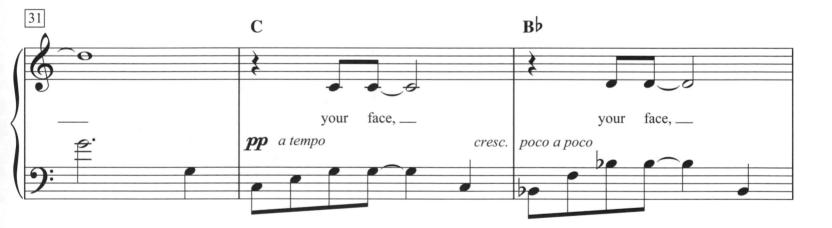

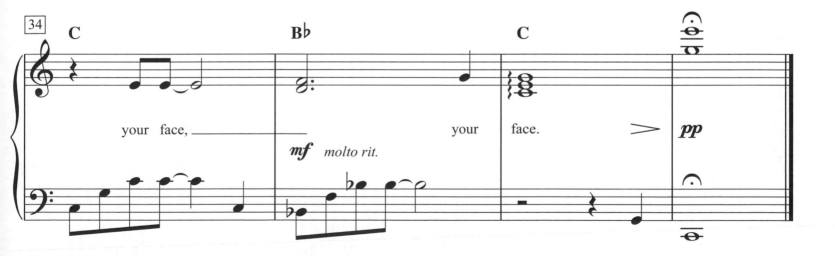

GOODBYE TO LOVE

Words and Music by RICHARD CARPENTER
and JOHN BETTIS
Arranged by Phillip Keveren

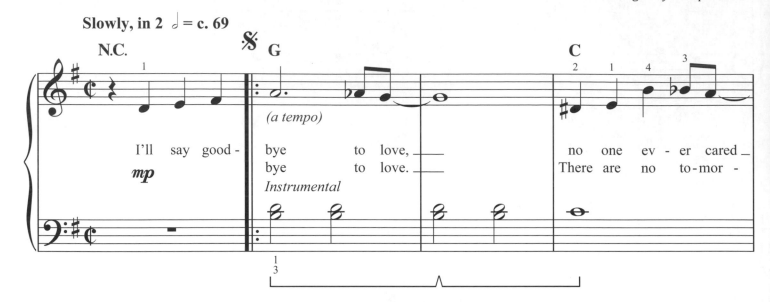

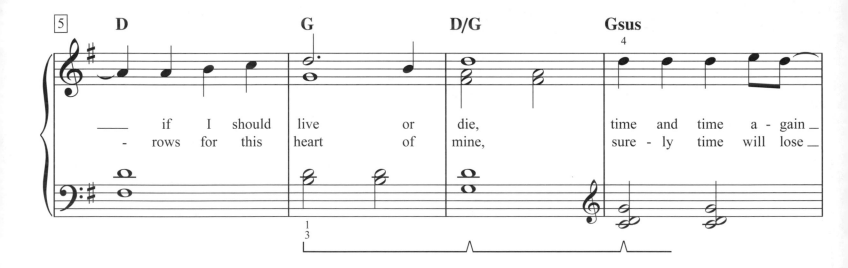

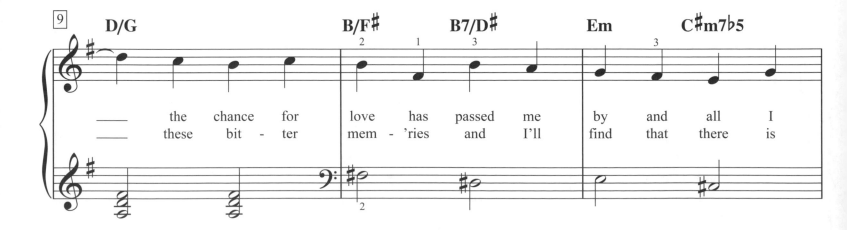

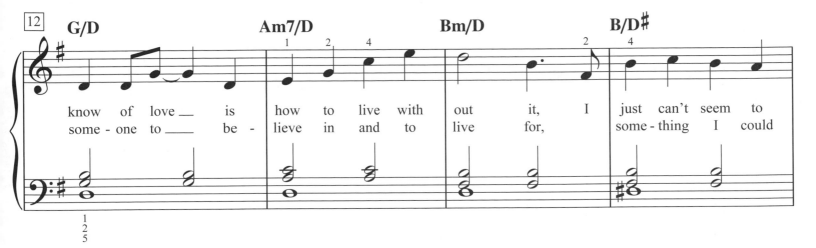

12 G/D · · · · · Am7/D · · · · Bm/D · · · B/D♯

know of love ___ is | how to live with | out it, I | just can't seem to
some - one to ___ be - | lieve in and to | live for, | some - thing I could

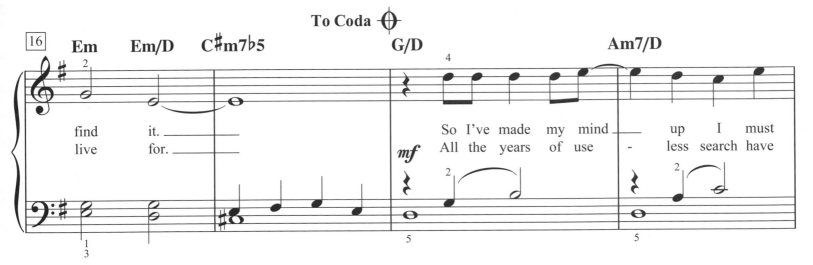

To Coda ⊕

16 Em · Em/D · C♯m7♭5 · · · G/D · · · Am7/D

find it. ___ | So I've made my mind ___ up I must
live for. ___ | All the years of use - less search have

mf

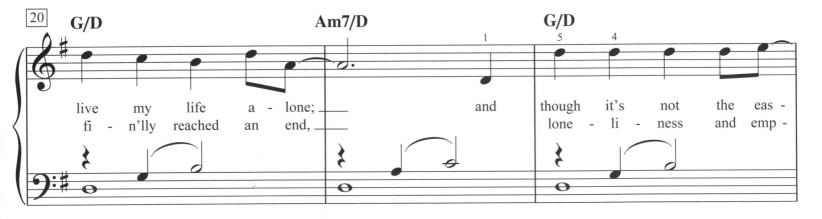

20 G/D · · · · · Am7/D · · · G/D

live my life a - lone; ___ | and | though it's not the eas -
fi - n'lly reached an end, ___ | | lone - li - ness and emp -

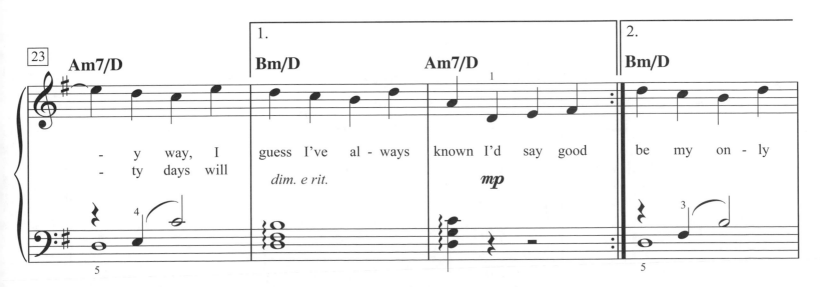

1.

23 Am7/D · · · · Bm/D · · · Am7/D · · · 2. Bm/D

- y way, I | guess I've al - ways | known I'd say good | be my on - ly
- ty days will | *dim. e rit.* | *mp*

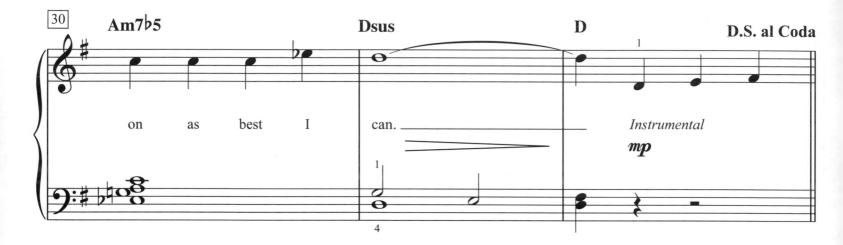

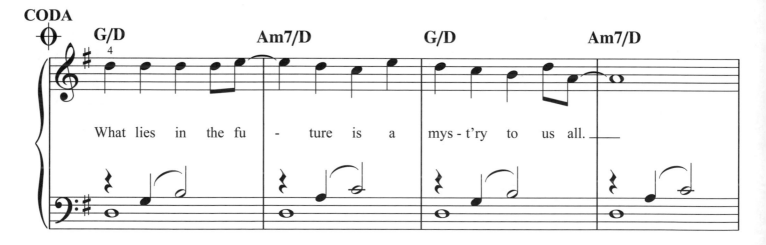

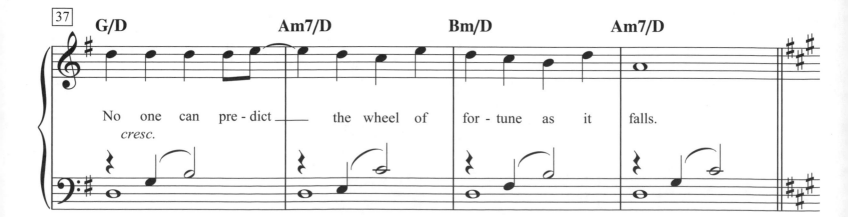

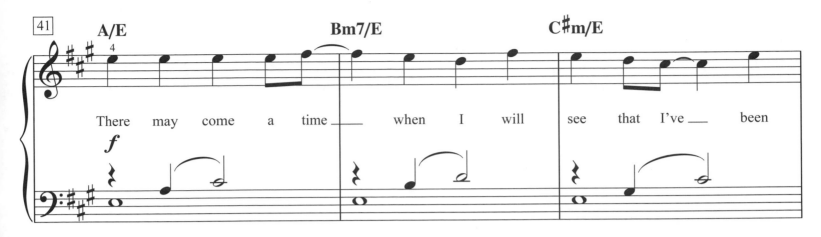

There may come a time ___ when I will see that I've ___ been

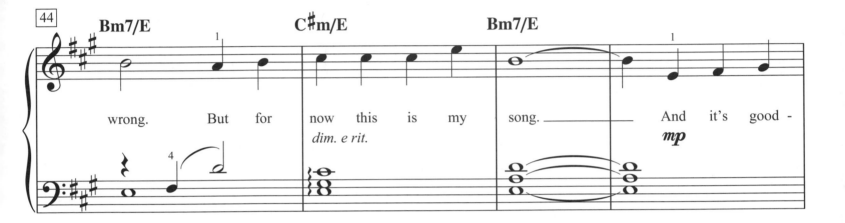

wrong. But for now this is my song. ___ And it's good -

dim. e rit.

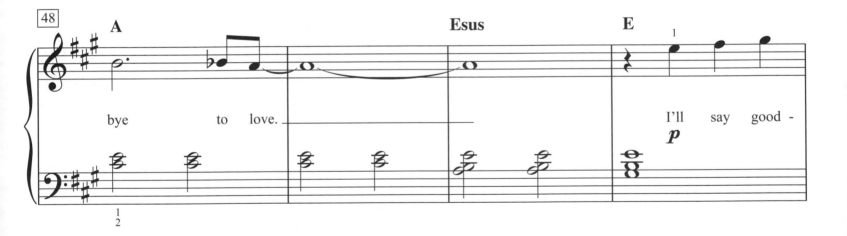

bye to love. ___ I'll say good -

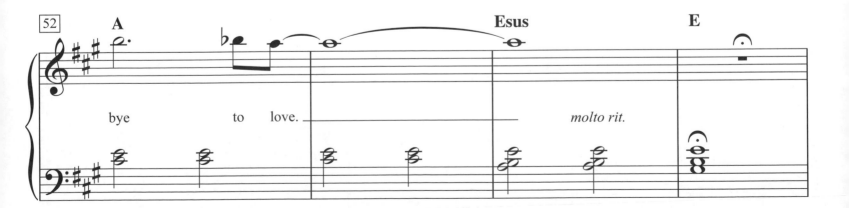

bye to love. ___ *molto rit.*

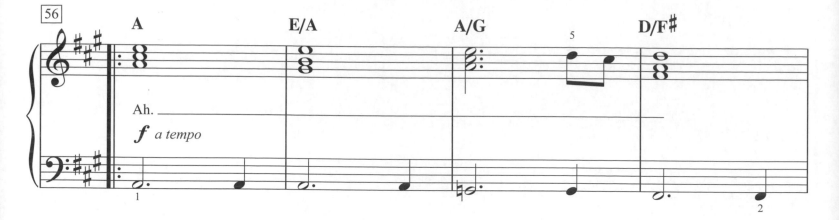

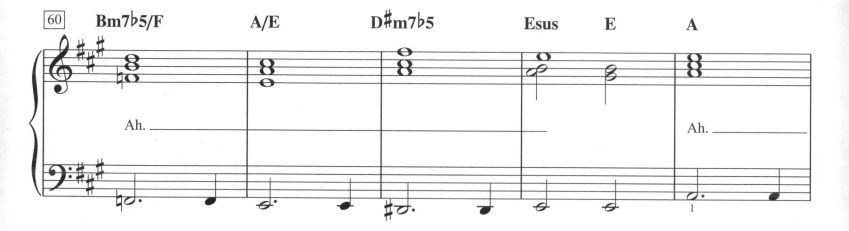

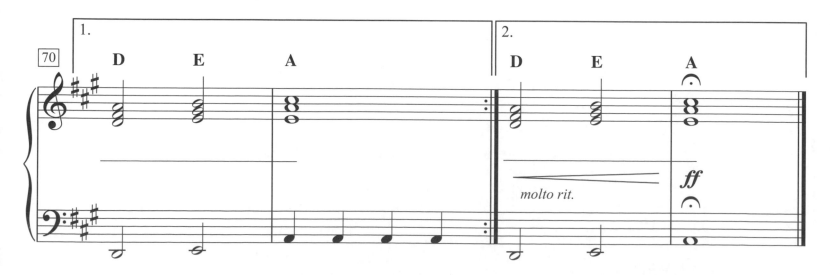

I WILL REMEMBER YOU

Theme from THE BROTHERS McMULLEN

Words and Music by SARAH McLACHLAN,
SEAMUS EGAN and DAVE MERENDA
Arranged by Phillip Keveren

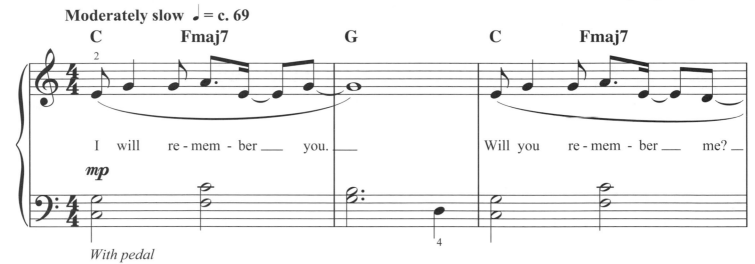

I will re-mem-ber ___ you. ___   Will you re-mem-ber ___ me? ___

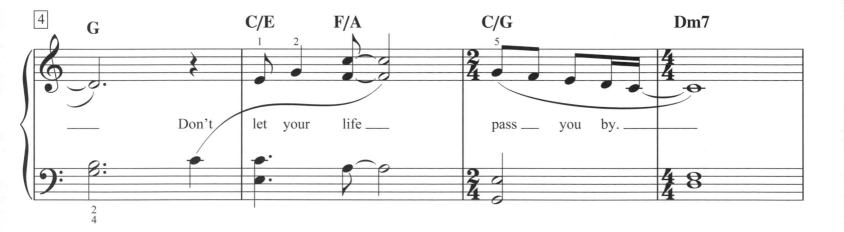

Don't let your life ___ pass ___ you by.

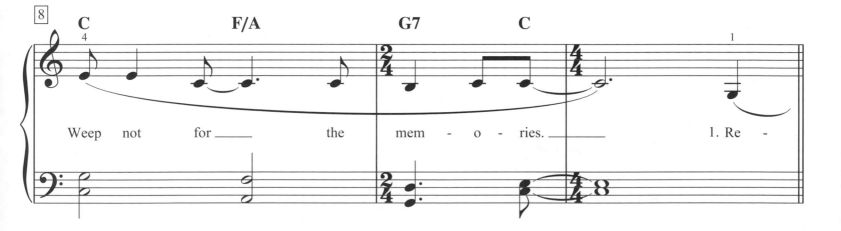

Weep not for ___ the mem - o - ries. ___   1. Re-

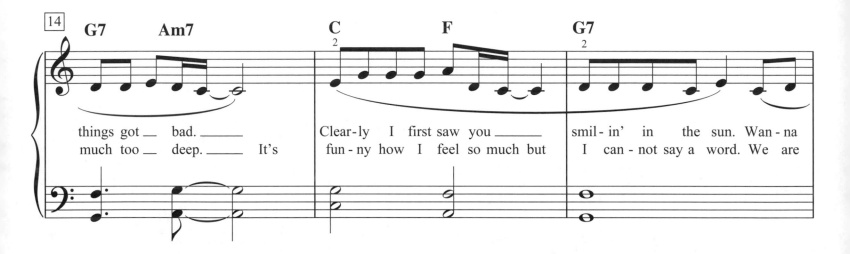

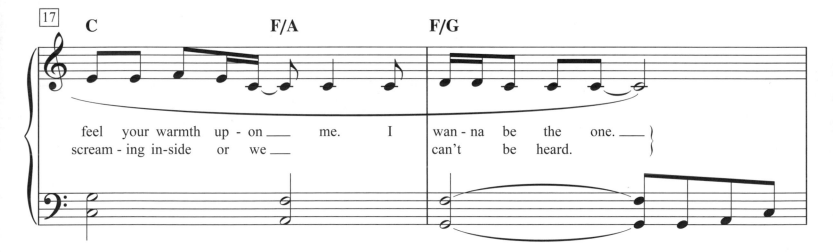

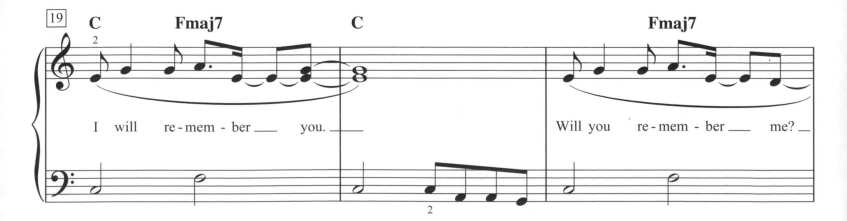

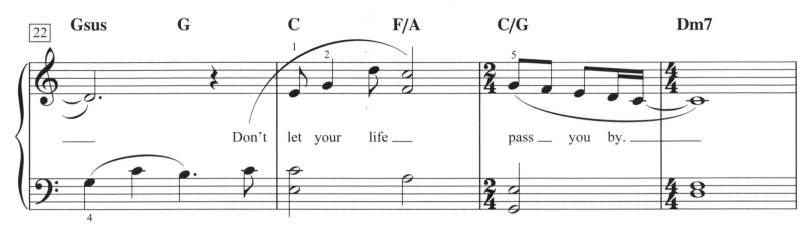

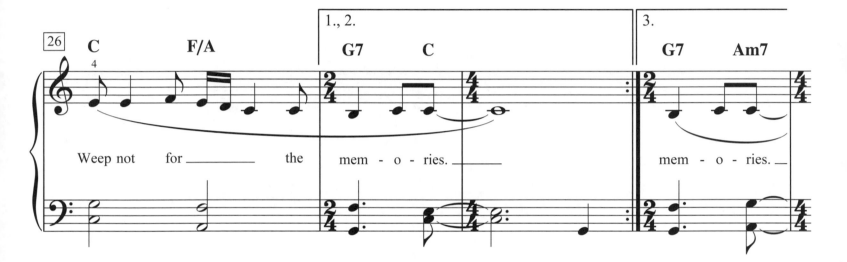

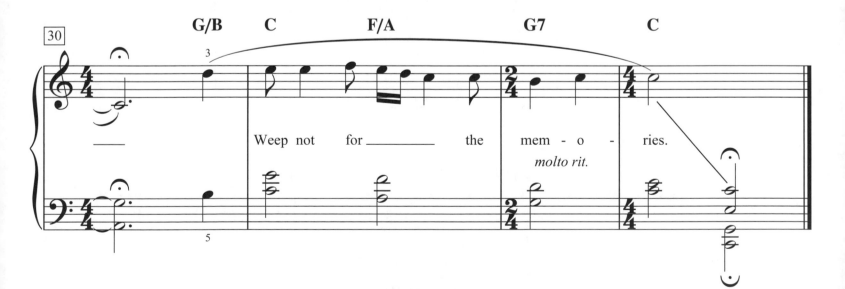

Additional Lyrics

3. I'm so afraid to love you, more afraid to lose you,
   Clinging to a past that doesn't let me choose.
   Well, once there was a darkness, a deep and endless night.
   You gave me ev'rything you had, oh, you gave me light.

HOME

Words and Music by AMY FOSTER-GILLIES,
MICHAEL BUBLÉ and ALAN CHANG
Arranged by Phillip Keveren

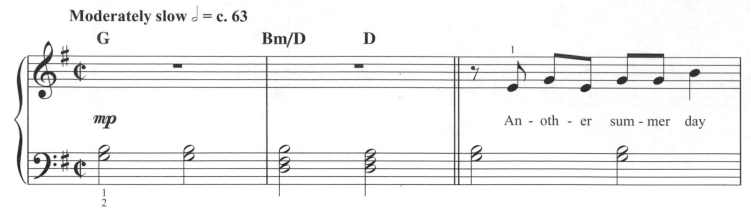

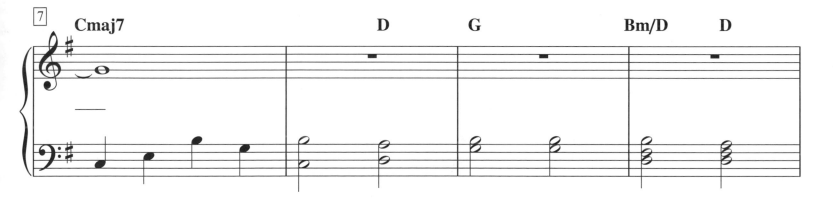

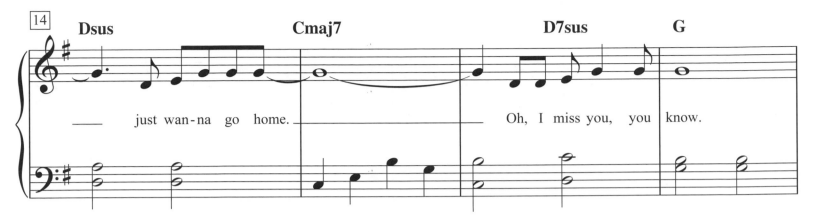

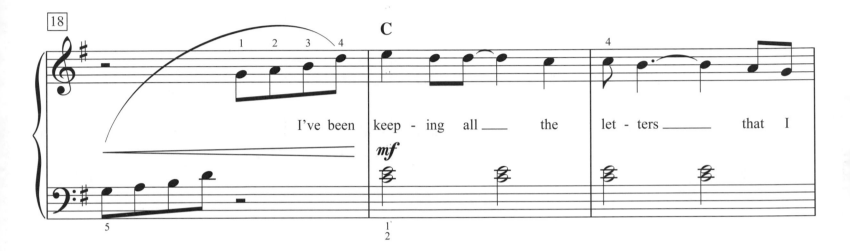

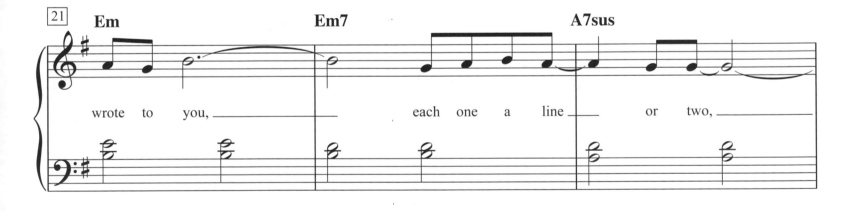

know that it's ___ just not e-nough. ___ My words were cold and flat, ___

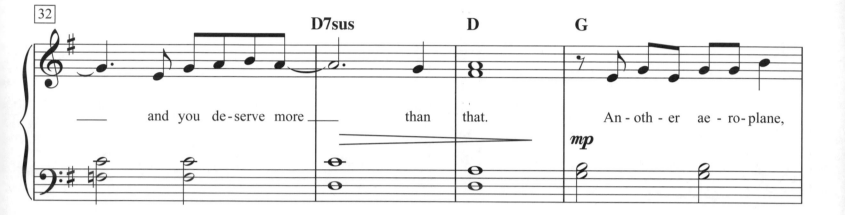

___ and you de-serve more ___ than that. An-oth-er ae-ro-plane,

an-oth-er sun-ny place; I'm luck-y, I know, ___ but I wan-na go home. ___

I've got to go home. Let me go

I WRITE THE SONGS

Words and Music by
BRUCE JOHNSTON
Arranged by Phillip Keveren

13 **F** **Gm7** **C7**

mf I write the songs __ that make the whole world sing; I write the songs __ of love and

16 **F** **Am7/E** **Dm** **Dm(maj7)** **Dm7** **G7sus** **G7**

spe - cial things. I write the songs __ that make the young girls cry. __

19 **Gm7/C** 1. **F7** **B♭m/F** **F**

I write the songs, __ I write the songs. __

2. 22 **F** **Esus** **E** **Em** **E**

__ Oh, my mu - sic makes you dance __ and gives you spir - it to take a chance,

with energy

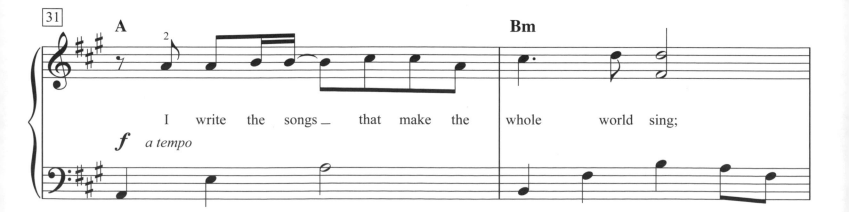

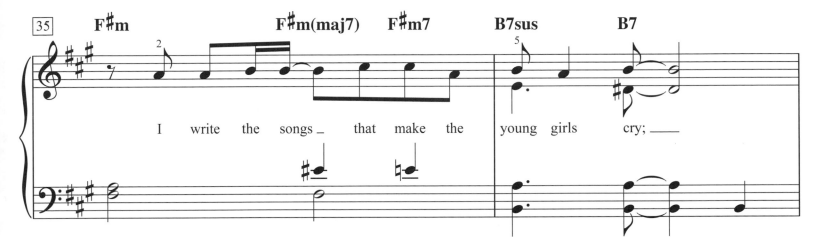

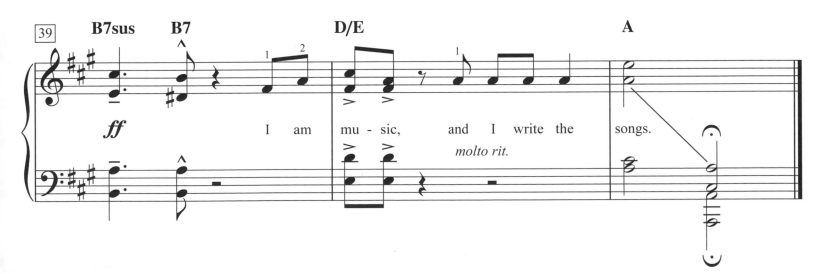

LADY IN RED

Words and Music by
CHRIS DeBURGH
Arranged by Phillip Keveren

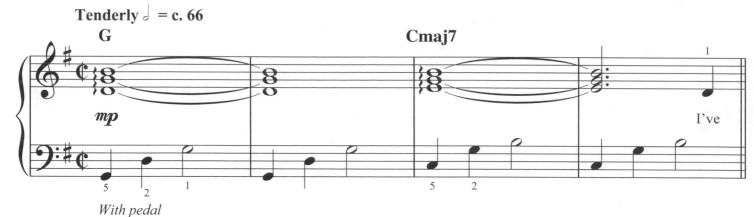

never seen you looking as love - ly as you did __ to - night; I've
never seen you looking so gor - geous as you did __ to - night; I've

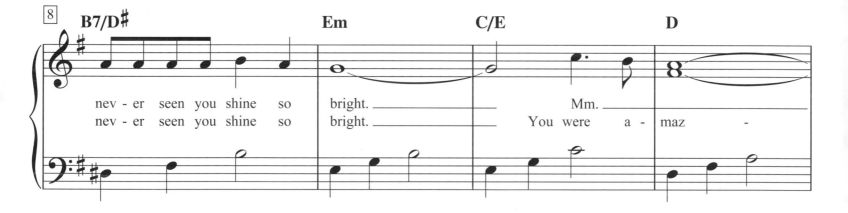

nev - er seen you shine so bright. _____ Mm.
nev - er seen you shine so bright. _____ You were a - maz -

____ ing. I've nev - er seen so man - y men ask ____ you if you want - ed to
ing. I've nev - er seen so man - y peo - ple want to be there ____ by your

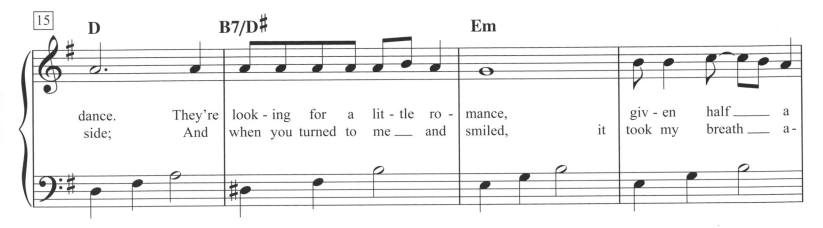

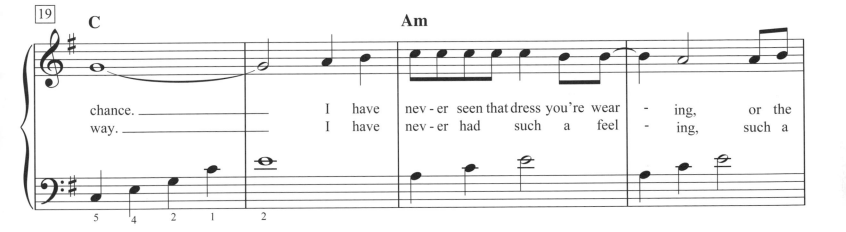

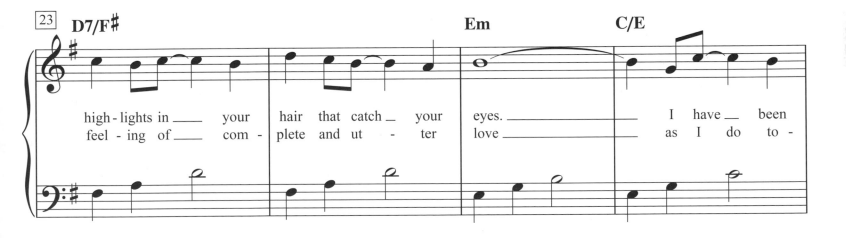

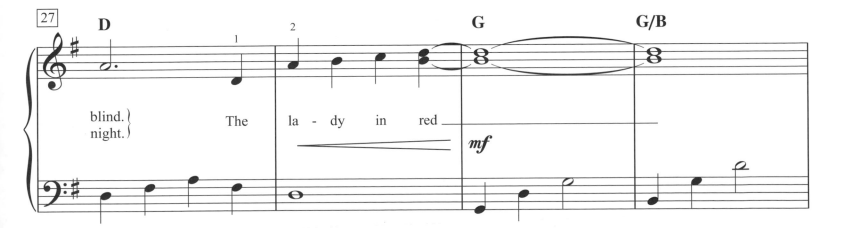

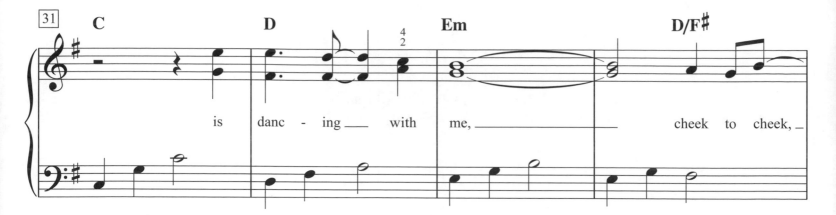

is danc - ing ___ with me, _____ cheek to cheek, __

___ There's no - bod - y here, _____ it's

just you and me. ___ It's where I wan - na be. But

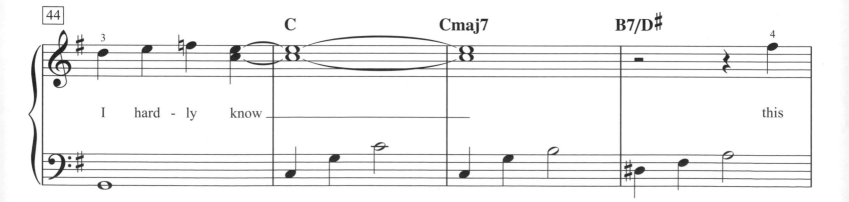

I hard - ly know _____ this

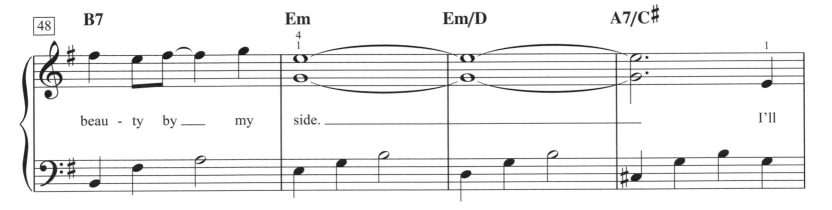

beau - ty by __ my side. _____ I'll

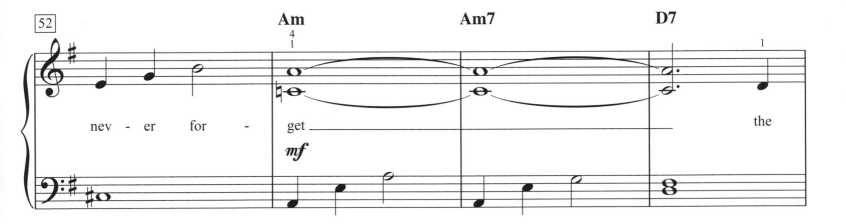

nev - er for - get _____ the

way you look __ to - night. I've

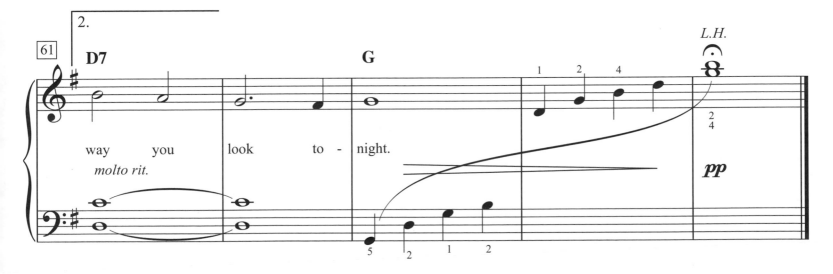

way you look to - night.

MY HEART WILL GO ON
(Love Theme From 'Titanic')
from the Paramount and Twentieth Century Fox Motion Picture TITANIC

Music by JAMES HORNER
Lyric by WILL JENNINGS
Arranged by Phillip Keveren

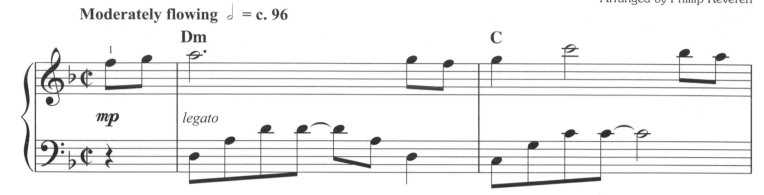

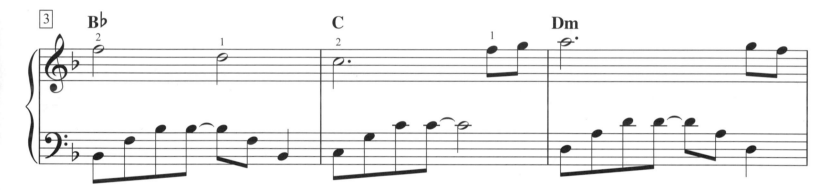

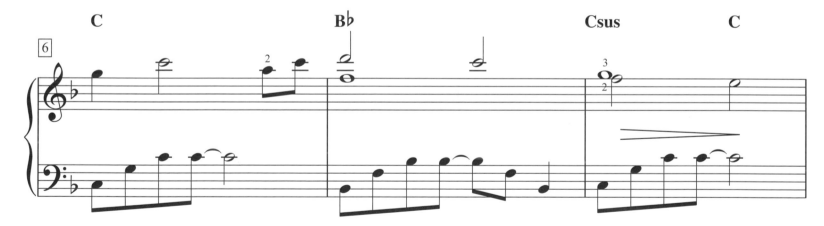

Ev - 'ry night in my dreams I see you, I
Love can touch us one time and last for a

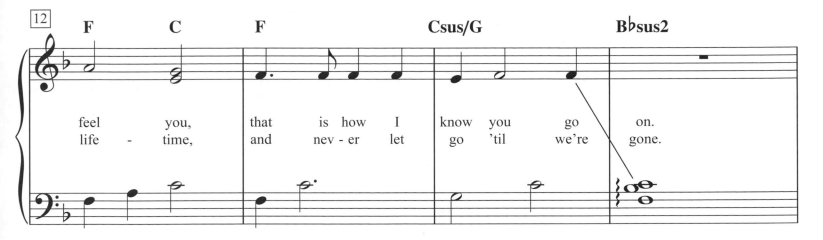

feel you, that is how I know you go on.
life - time, and nev - er let go 'til we're gone.

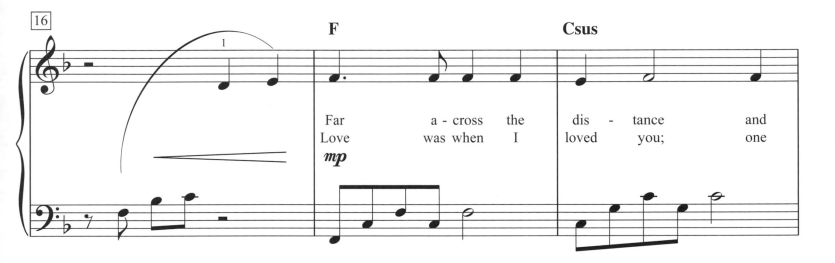

Far a - cross the dis - tance and
Love was when I loved you; one

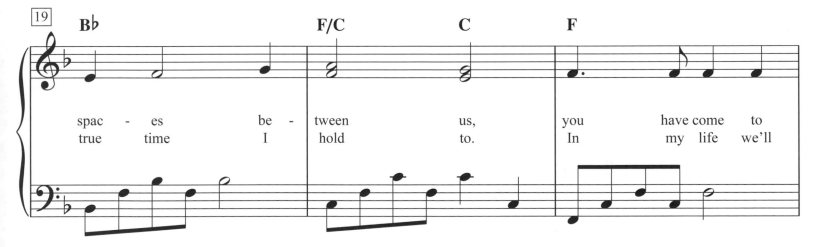

spac - es be - tween us, you have come to
true time I hold us to. In my life we'll

show you go on.
al - ways go on.

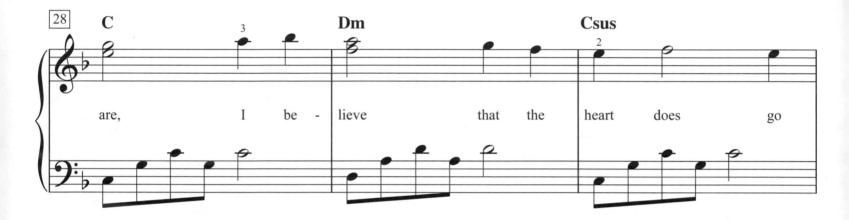

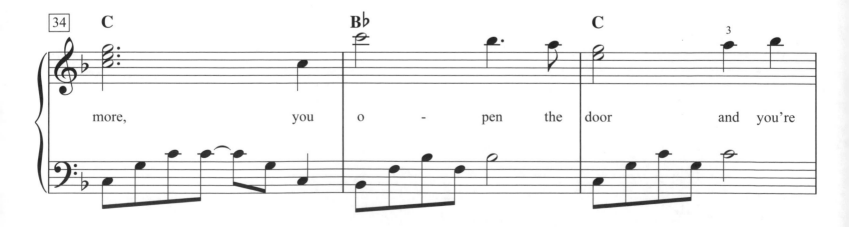

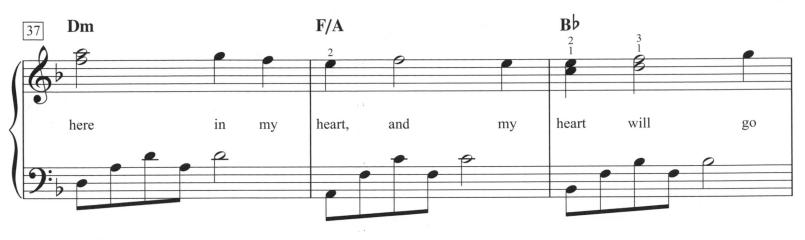

here in my heart, and my heart will go

on and on.

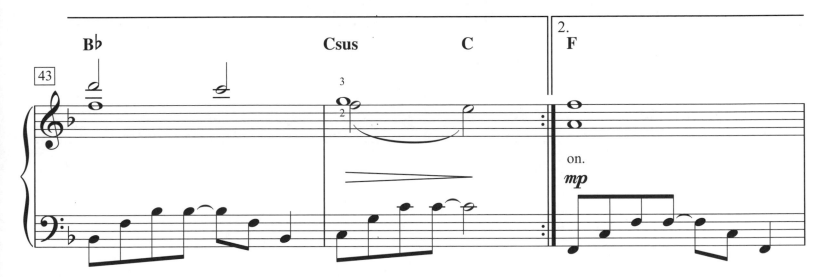

on.

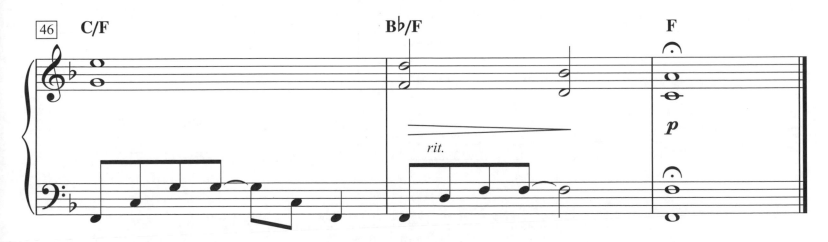

PERFECT

Words and Music by ED SHEERAN
Arranged by Phillip Keveren

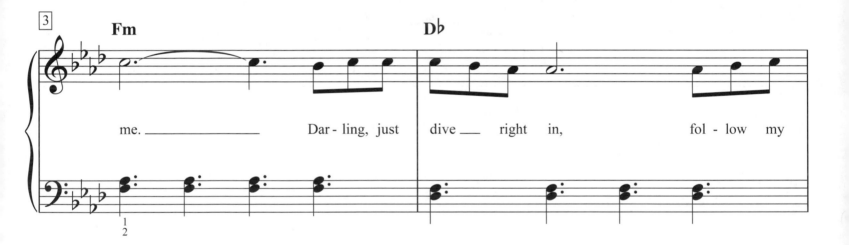

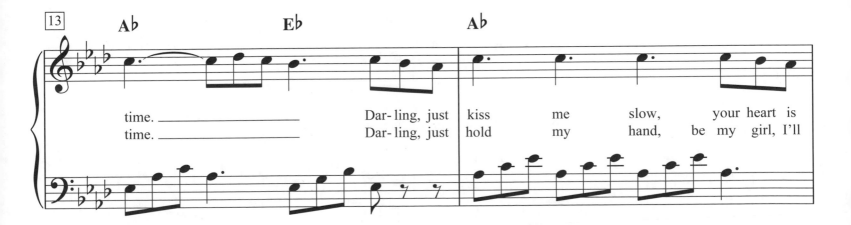

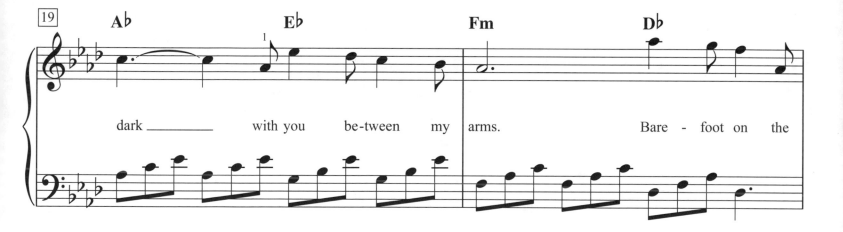

To Coda

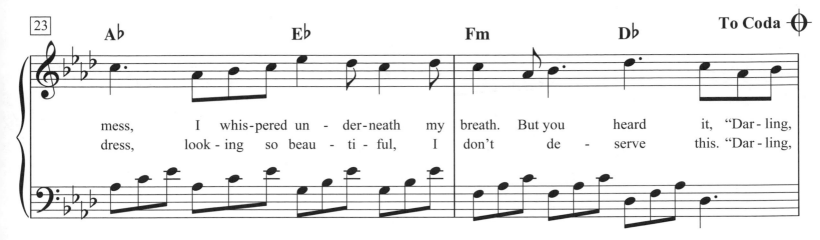

mess, I whis-pered un - der-neath my | breath. But you heard it, "Dar - ling,
dress, look - ing so beau - ti - ful, I | don't de - serve this. "Dar - ling,

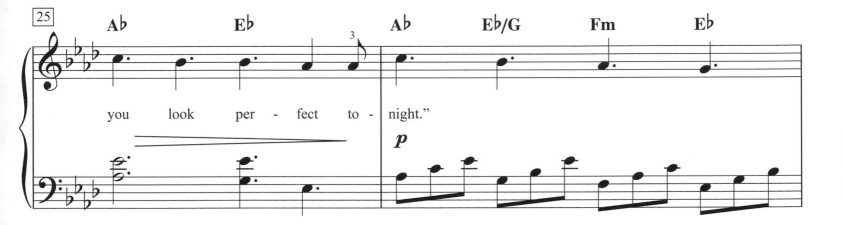

you look per - fect to - | night."

p

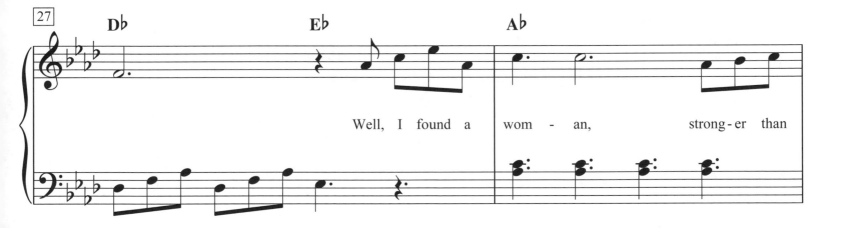

Well, I found a | wom - an, strong - er than

an - y - one I know. ___ She shares my | dreams, I hope that some - day I'll share her

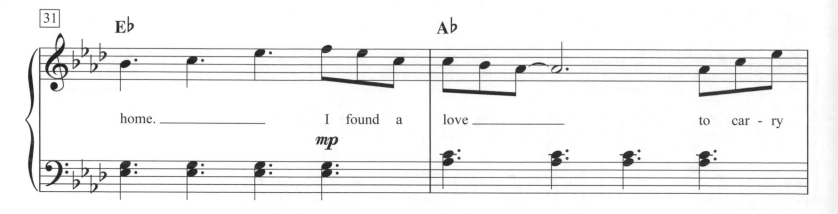

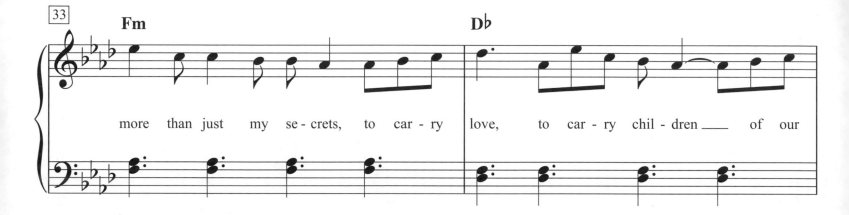

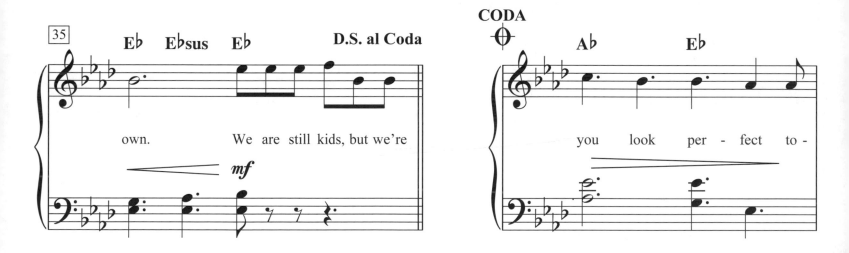

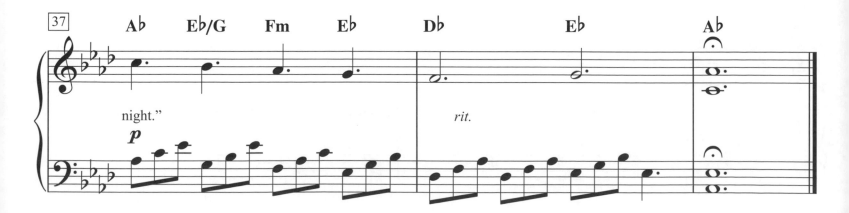

RAINDROPS KEEP FALLIN' ON MY HEAD

from BUTCH CASSIDY AND THE SUNDANCE KID

Lyrics by HAL DAVID
Music by BURT BACHARACH
Arranged by Phillip Keveren

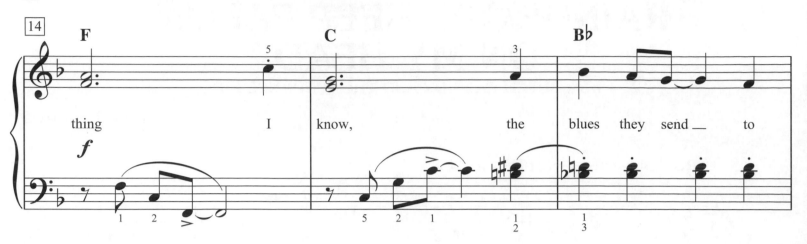

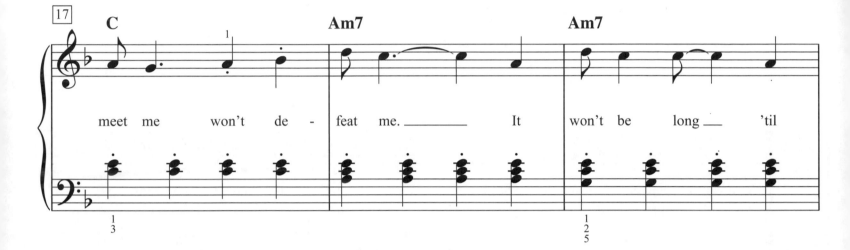

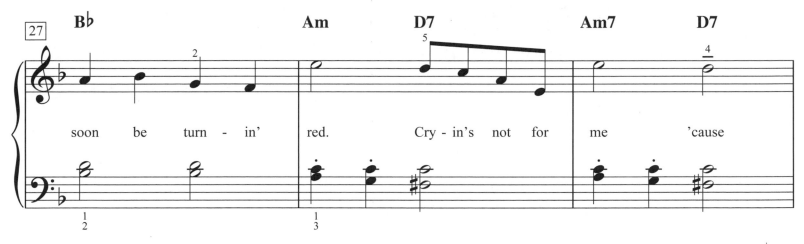

soon be turn - in' red. Cry - in's not for me 'cause

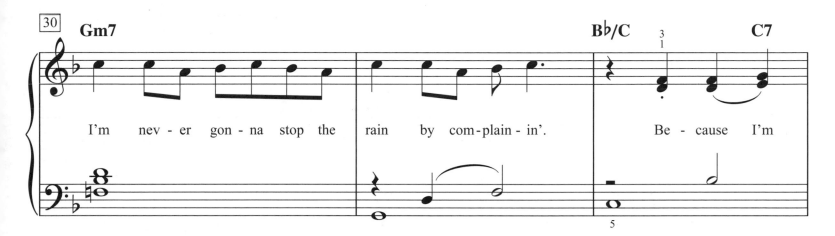

I'm nev - er gon - na stop the rain by com-plain - in'. Be - cause I'm

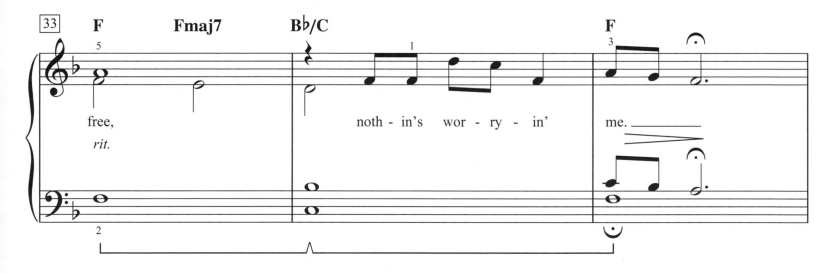

free, nothin's wor - ry - in' me.

rit.

mf a tempo

p

A THOUSAND YEARS

from the Summit Entertainment film THE TWILIGHT SAGA: BREAKING DAWN - PART 1

Words and Music by DAVID HODGES
and CHRISTINA PERRI
Arranged by Phillip Keveren

Tenderly ♩. = 46–48

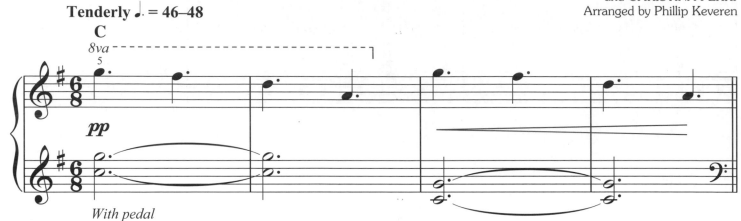

Heart beats fast. Col - ors and prom - is -
Time stands still. Beau - ty in all she

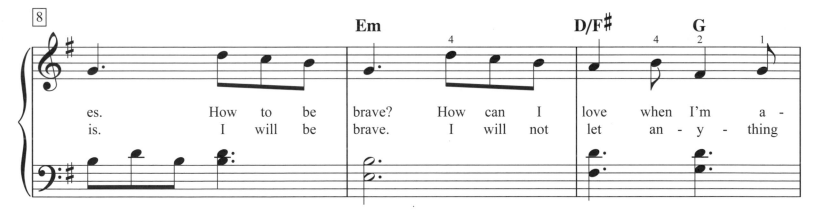

es. How to be brave? How can I love when I'm a -
is. I will be brave. I will not let an - y - thing

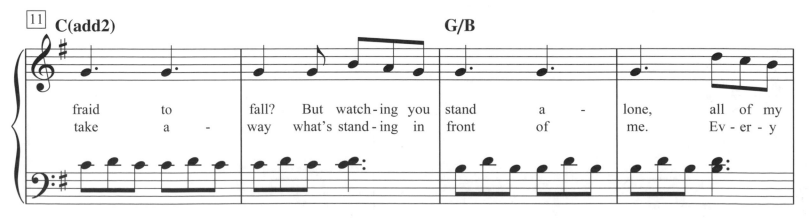

fraid to fall? But watch - ing you stand a - lone, all of my
take a - way what's stand - ing in front of me. Ev - er - y

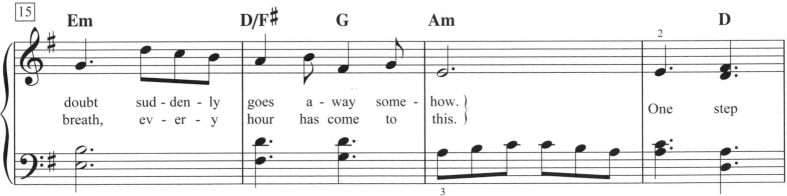

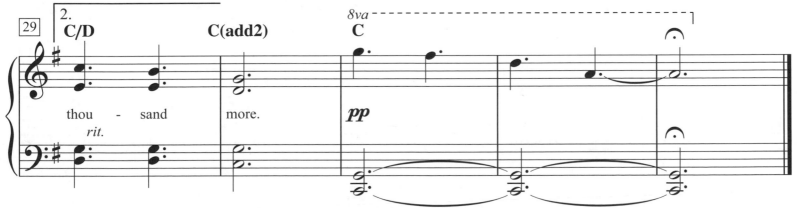

RIGHT HERE WAITING

Words and Music by RICHARD MARX
Arranged by Phillip Keveren

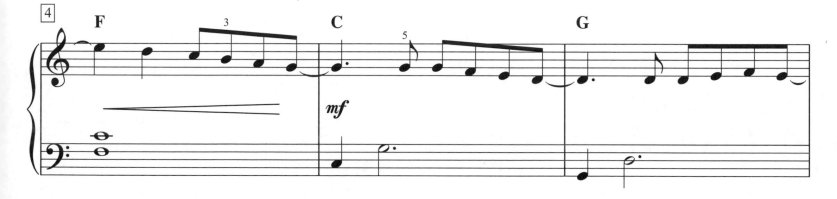

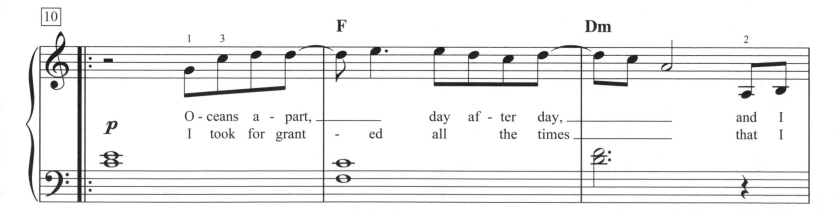

O - ceans a - part, _____ day af - ter day, _____ and I
I took for grant - ed all the times _____ that I

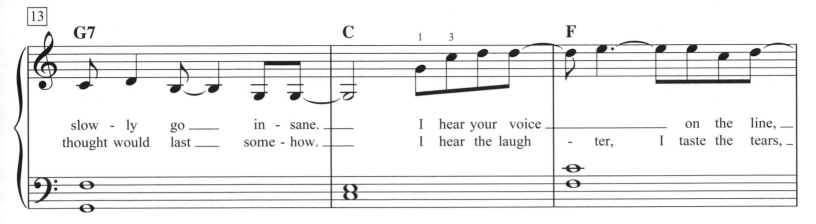

13 G7 — C — F

slow - ly go ___ in - sane. ___ I hear your voice ___ on the line, ___
thought would last ___ some - how. ___ I hear the laugh - ter, I taste the tears, ___

16 Dm — G7 — Am

___ but it does - n't stop ___ the pain. ___ If I see you next ___
___ but I can't get near ___ you now. Oh, can't you see ___

cresc.

19 Dm — Am — Dm7 — G7

___ to nev - er, how can we say ___ for - ev - er?
___ it, ba - by? You've got me go - in' cra - zy.

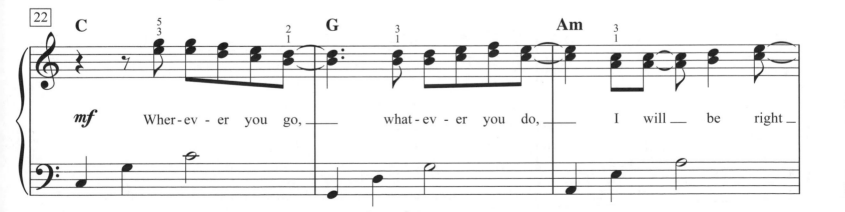

22 C — G — Am

mf Wher - ev - er you go, ___ what - ev - er you do, ___ I will ___ be right

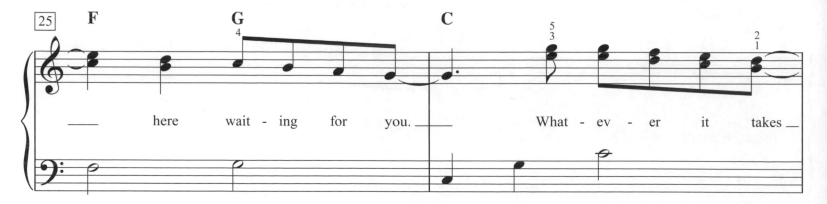

here wait - ing for you. Whatev - er it takes

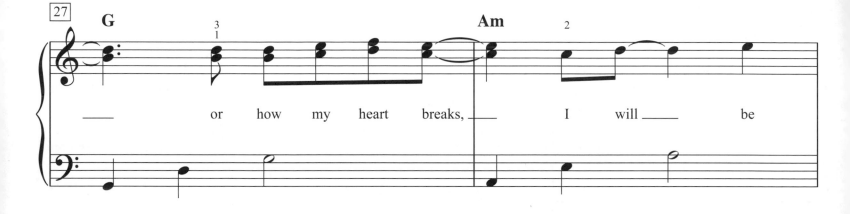

or how my heart breaks, I will be

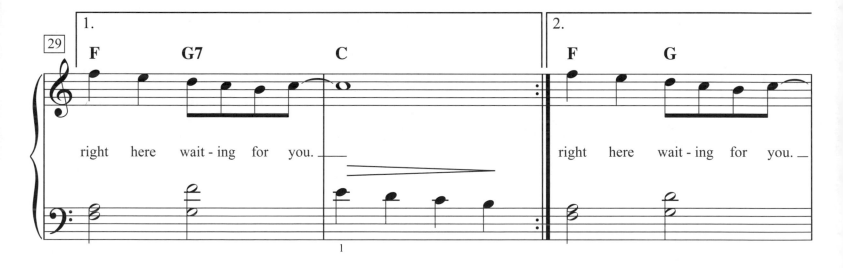

right here wait - ing for you. right here wait - ing for you.

Right here wait - ing for you.

rit.